# Kitchen Abrasives

Laura Klinkon

Stesichorus  Publications

# Acknowledgments

"Two and Two and Two," Parts One and Two, were performed October 13, 2012 by Andy Doyle accompanied on piano by Jean Vogdes Callahan, in Episode 25 of the online The Cakewalk Show, Ithaca, N.Y.; "Cinnamon rings" appeared in the December 2013 Canto Magazine online; "Two and Two and Two" was read March 11, 2014 at Writers and Books, Rochester, N.Y. as part of the Genesee Reading Series; "In a hurry" was published in the Le Mot Juste 2015 yearly anthology; "Salt potato" and "I don't intend to be artsy-fartsy" were read October 12, 2014 and February 1, 2015 at Books Etc. in Macedon, N.Y. as part of the series "Poetry as Philosophy," featuring the author along with poet/philosopher David White; additional poems from the present collection were read February 22, 2015 at St. John Fisher College, Skalny Welcome Center, sponsored by Rochester Poets; "Cranberries numinous" and "Wholeness" were aired June 23, 2016 on the Flower City YAWP poetry program, hosted by Albert Abonado of Writers and Books, on 104.3FM WAYO, Rochester, N.Y.

Thanks to all! In addition, I would like to thank my Collision Art and Philosophy friends for their continued encouragement and support, as well as Just Poets workshop members who enthusiastically offered feedback on several of these poems.

Copyright © 2017 by Laura Klinkon
All rights reserved. No portion of this work may be reproduced or transmitted in any form or by any means, electronic or mechanical, including photocopying and recording, or by any information storage and retrieval system, without written permission from the author.

Cover art by Peter Klinkon
Design Consultation: Editions Printing

Published by Stesichorus Publications, Rochester, N.Y.

ISBN: 978-0-9986405-0-1
First Edition

# Kitchen Abrasives

Laura Klinkon

Kubla Khan, euphoric:

"....my empire is made of the stuff of crystals, its molecules arranged in a perfect pattern. Amid fermenting elements, a hard splendid diamond takes shape, an immense, faceted, transparent mountain.... Why do you linger over inessential melancholies?"

Italo Calvino, *Invisible Cities*

# Contents

| | |
|---|---|
| Introduction | 9 |
| I keep wondering | 11 |
| Cinnamon rings | 12 |
| Salt potato | 13 |
| Cocktail bottle | 14 |
| Cranberries numinous | 15 |
| In a hurry | 16 |
| Two and Two and Two | 17 |
| Sort of what? | 23 |
| I don't intend to be artsy-fartsy | 25 |
| Cold feet | 27 |
| Wholeness | 29 |
| Flies 2014 | 31 |
| The birds have returned | 32 |
| A lightening bug upon my shoulder | 33 |
| Fainthearted flies 2015 | 34 |
| Evening star | 35 |
| Laptop | 36 |
| Mirror on the wall | 37 |
| Writing is my therapy | 39 |
| Surprise of the flies 2016 | 41 |

# Introduction

My poetry professor at American University (a Pulitzer Prize winner,* though he wasn't at the time) told me that to him my poems echo the phrase "I know." I still wonder what he meant by this because what always strikes me is how much I don't know, and I do believe many of my poems reflect the effort to know or to build some structure around things or ideas that I haven't yet figured out. It's like E.M. Forster who said, "How do I know what I think until I see what I say?" One could also ask, How do I know what I'll say until I think it? or better yet, How do I know what I'll say until I write it? Er...this is getting confusing.

Which leads me to another place my poems may be coming from: confusion. In general, I do believe confusion is a starting point for many poems. Perhaps especially the poems that are humorous or trying to be. After all, confusion is funny. Imagine someone who is wearing a heavy hat in summer. He's dying to take it off, because he's hot. But somehow any place or surface nearby that could accommodate the hat, doesn't seem at all appropriate. No, not the table on the sunny patio, not the bench by the side of the pool. No, not even the St. John's Wort bush beside the veranda. You can see him running around brandishing his hat in search of a place to put it, sweating and swearing in his disconcerting confusion. A weirdly exaggerated example? Weird exaggeration combined with confusion is all the funnier, I think. Maybe not raucously funny. But... gently abrasive?

In the present collection much of the confusion is expressed with regard to things rather than people. On top of that, I express my conundra by way of words...that mainly only further confuse. So, if you laugh at these poems, it will be a chuckle at most, caused by your own confusion, mine, or by your recognition that confusion is clearly inevitable.

Should I go on and explain each poem and how it connects to my thesis? I think I'll let you do it. I would invite you to write me with your explanations, but you may not be comfortable with your own confusion and resent me, or you may be annoyed by my poems' tentative resolutions. So please don't raise my already intense level of confusion. Enjoy the poems, or, if not, just deal with it!

Laura Klinkon, December 2016

*Henry S. Taylor, winner, Pulitzer Prize for Poetry 1986.

**I keep wondering**

I keep wondering
why pineapple stings raw
why figs too many prickle
why thistle, stubborn, stays
what bromide has to do
with bromelain or bromine
and psoralen with umbelli-
ferone and how milk
can be seltzed from thistle
and why not.

## Cinnamon rings

Cinnamon, accustomed from its marrow days
to sizzle through tree rings all the way to their outer
rough-hewn coil may at long last flavor rings of Saturn
before micro-milling or dissolving in icy vertigo. Yet—
odds are, it will sooner spiral in metabolic,
day-old dunes to become a jurassical
fossil in an old familiar pit.

## Salt potato

Consider the salt potato, the humble
member of the potassial array
alongside its sweet and pointed, or
red or yellow bulbous brothers,
the batata, the yuca, the yam.
Does it grow in salt marshes?
Is the taste ultra-savory au naturel? Or,
conversely, unpalatable without salt?
Truly, its main features are its small,
smooth, oval/size, carressible, shape—
fitting quite nicely into one's cupped palm—
snug, but cozier when still warm. So,
where is the salt? In the skin that perhaps
preserves its natural dole? A peel you mustn't
or needn't remove? Is it that, rolling,
it easily drops its earthly salts? Or
picks up more? Does it release its salts
to the cooking broth? What, really,
do we know about it? There may be
Ayurvedic properties, like rubbing
on the body to neutralize perspirative
toxic salts! Round and smooth and
small could also have appeal of organ-
icity—like babies' toes. Shall I admit
my knowledge of why salt? is small potatoes?
or...do a phrasal search for "salt of the earth"
or, er..."potassium chloride"...?

**The cocktail bottle**

The cocktail sauce, much smaller than the ketchup,
looks on dismayed, worried we could eat
more shell fish than Knackwurst.

## Cranberries numinous

The number of frozen cranberries
to drop into your cereal
depends upon the numinous number
of your astrological house, as
any certified seer will tell you.

Mine is in the third house,
meaning I should pop in three—
a disappointing, miserly number,
which I adjust—at first by adding
three again—except that, the number six,

residing in the sixth house, and having
a negative numen, must be counter-
balanced by one more—making seven
cranberries—and returning positive
karma, delightfully, to my buckwheat.

I'll not disclose the zodiacal
signs these numbers represent,
as this may prejudice your opinion
and upset your focus on this key
calculation, you fully knowing your sign,
though not your house assignation.

In time, you'll retrieve this datum to
reckon how many cranberries are
cosmically optimal: why I'm advocating—
no, illuminating—this foolproof algorithm.
Depending on your sign and ingenuity,
you could garner cranberries galore,
while merely experimenting!

It's a celestial, dawn-delivered formula
for beginning your day—unless, be warned,
you're adding blueberries which if dreamed of
beforehand, simply cannot be computed, for
they obfuscate decision making, placing
you, ominously, on the dark side of the moon.

**In a hurry**

Shoes, please untie while I do my makeup.
Napkin, blot my lips as I change my socks.
Slacks, pull up, while my blouse is buttoning.
Roll back, sleeves, you're a bit too long.

Teapot, bubble—and don't get cooler.
Timer, crank a few notches and chime at three.
Lovely pekoe, spoon in a fresh infusion.
Cup and strainer do your thing.

Fridge, wake up and jog my memory,
what I need to buy today.
Pencil, write it on the notepad up there.
Stick it in my grocery net, okay?

## Two and Two and Two

At one job there was
A department
Head who just
Could not tolerate
Duplicate cups
On a secretary's
Desk—sign of
A sloppy mind
Or some such;
"Nobody needs
Two mugs."

This dictum
Often has
Weighed upon
My psyche—especially
When as
Now at home
Appear two,
Then two, then
Two, so that I've
Come to want to
Understand the
Nature of the vice
Involved.

Two cans of Comet
In the powder/shower room:
One taped down, the
Other ready to shake—
Makes
Sense to me;
If the open one gets wet,
The other's dry and handy—
Right on the toilet tank.
Two hand towels—one
Clean, one going—

No time lost between
Towels—plus you have
One for
Cursory dryings, one
For thorough—
Bonus boon!

Next door in
Mom's room—Two bottles of
Ginger ale—one full,
The other half—
Destined to be replaced
Without a glitch—or
Trip to the
Kitchen.

Two pillows: one for the
Head, second for feet—
The first sometimes doing
Double duty, when the other's
Not so pleasant;
Two sets of shoes—one left to dry
If I've walked into the shower
Without thinking
And one
To walk over
The inevitably dusty floor.

So, this boss of ours
Wasn't perfectly savvy—
Didn't think much
About contingencies;
Not a Noah, who, for sure,
Knew:
You have to have two
And two, and two—
Just in case.

**Part Two**

I have other things
In pairs that
Go beyond contingency:
Two vials of shampoo, one
Thick and viscous, the other
Watered down—it suds up
So much faster! And up the
Stairs,
Two coffee cans to toss
Kitchen scraps—one
For grinds intended
For earth directly, one for
Bits to compost.

And, I always buy
Two bananas
One for mashing,
One for knoshing.
What do I not have
Two of?!!
Two kinds of fish,
Two kinds of
Chocolate powder,
Oats rolled and
Oat bran,
And in the sitting room and
Social area,
Two kinds of media access,
Two main friends—
And yes,
I even have
Two sons—plus
Two future
Daughters-in-law
With two grandchild possibilities.

What ol' May-Not-Have-Two-Of
Didn't see: Two does have serendipity.
My Lord, by now,
I surely can deflect
Those grievous lingering stares!
Quoting from Number Two Himself:
"Where two or more are gathered...
there will I be also."

Hmm, actually that
Would make three...
So, going back to our
Boss...

**Part Three A**

Surely, he wouldn't
Have agreed there should
Be three, and yet since often
There are,
As in my house
The third and private tier,
I take this chance to show
That even within three, two mainly allows
For privacy—
A double bed, a double dresser
Double closet divided for two;
Two small windows,
Two secondary rooms—
For in our second decade, we want
Our own of things,
Households ending up with four,
Even the doors—Because, there needs to
Be a linen closet. (The bathroom's pairing
With the powder/shower room's downstairs).

How did that man dare or did he just not care
That human beings always
Fare better with some time

Away from stares or
To practice solemn prayer.
Had he never heard of God?
Or Freud?

**Part Three B**

There is a thought I
Mustn't lose, that
Nature is made up of
Twos—which our world
Reflects creating
Grace and awesome
Symmetry—I fear
Most don't really
See the wonderness
Of existentiality
Embodied in the number
Two and sometimes
Three.
Think Eyes, Ears.
Legs, Knees—and even
Double/Singular anomalies
Like the navel, with both
Ins
And Outs!—Not to be silly,
But, reflecting on Freud,
We have conscious
And sub-conscious—or Jung's
Thinking and feeling, or
Politics and its polarities
Or beauty calculated in the
Golden mean—There's earth, there's sky,
There's land and water, or
You yourself
Reflected in the latter. Now,
How do you suppose
The parallel universe idea arose?
You see where thoughts of two
May lead?

Well. Could this consequence
Explain why our old boss was pained
By twain? Didn't care to
Have one see the multifariousness
Of two or three, because
He needed you to stay on chore,
Without redounding to your inner
Core, that he and job were awful bores?

Contingency, serendipity,
Privacy, and existentiality
Were four
Abhorrent elements
He couldn't let you shore—his own
Work: to nurture and ensure
Eventual numbers two,
Both staid and true—like him
And possibly, though doubtfully,
You.

## Sort of what?

A sort is one of those things
we hardly speak of. I mean, really,
what is a sort? Well, it's a sort
of a sort of a something! Hmm, a bit blurry like
Sambo's tigers, 'til it all turns into golden ghee.
Okay, it's a kind. Kind? It's not kind at all,
especially since, "sort" doesn't tell you it's
something you need to work at, think about,
figure out—to understand it—which is one of
the problems. I mean, if you embark on a piece
of work, you should know what the canoe will
hold and where it's going.

In America and globally now,
there's no such thing as a sort, but only sorting.
For the reason that it's better
if you see yourself just going along. Asking
about the end product, would raise its value
(while possibly sinking yours). So, sorting
papers is a paper sort, sorting buttons,
a button sort, sorting socks, a sock sort. All
these sorts boxed, wrapped, and sold are worth
their weight in gold. Especially, if the box,
the inside wrap, and outside wrap come with!
But we live in caboodles equipped with flow—
better to toe the line sorting any sort of thing,
than to sort out what it is we're making.

Of course, important sorts are done by
machines who mind their business.
The worker standing by just checks if
the machine knows what it's doing:
checkers I think they're called, who with their
high-grade smarts could be checking anywhere,
anything. So, you see, a sort also requires a check
(something "sorting" doesn't say). And

when you get a good sort, that should raise the value! By contrast, a box of dried or burnt-up raisins isn't worth the check you're paid!

If someone says, I have to do a pile of sorting, I get the shivers, because there's lots more to a sort than meets the eye, and it's largely unnoticed, unappreciated labor—why I avoid my sorting like the dickens—until I think of the sort I'll end up with and, in advance, buy me a raisin pie or pecan ice cream or some other kind reward.

## I don't intend to be artsy-fartsy

I don't intend to be artsy-fartsy
yet I can't seem to help it
for I do make art whenever I eat
or plan a meal. You won't find
a form more interesting, substance
more engaging, movement more
dynamic than in your G.I. tube.
You only need to trans-substantiate
its fabric, imagine it transparent,
see the contours, colors, textures
as they flow right through.

My lentil-chicken soup in browns
and whites and somewhat green,
meandering, leaping like an autumn brook,
made a mental tapestry today, and
was a gentle visitor to my gastroroom—
a sand-dollar cookie and
lemon-ginger tea came, too.

Today I will not think about the sculpture
that I'll make for dinner—dynamic and
impromptu also go together! Well,
the possibilities are endless, and
honestly this concept could improve
your taste—besides your diet.

Yesterday we visited an Ethiopian
buffet. You look at the colors of that
food and arrange them in the strata
you contrive: deep green, cyclamen red,
tiger-lily coral. High summer—
which could easily turn to early spring—
depending on your preferences.

What good is a sculpture you can't see?

you ask. What good is a sculpture
you can't digest? Visualize it
in your mind! You've created, pre-
conceived it, with all the wealth of content
available to you—three times a day, all in
absorbing play—both good and good, I'd say!

## Cold feet

I have cold feet
quickly gliding
over the kitchen
floor to the fridge
to grab a pickle
in hope it will suffice—
I happen to be
hungry, but do not
want to make a full
meal. I didn't even
bother to pull on my
socks—more hungry
than cold...for a while.

Somehow I like
maintaining cold feet
as a testament to those
who've gone before and
those who still do—I walk
in their feet as it were: Indian
maidens tripping through
corn fields, shepherds
with lost soles, arctic
wanderers—more cold
than hungry, South American
kids, who'll need pair after
pair if they can only get
the first one, other reality
people made stronger
each day, from the feet up.

Mine are nearly
clay now as callouses
accumulate—in winter
I don't de-calcify—a
precaution in the event
an intruder compels me to

hurry barefoot out the door
in snow or over the icy
pavement. I like to think
my feet are tempered
by frequent sliding
over cold tile and ready for
anything.

My dad required serious
pedicures—I should have
paid attention; I'm sure
I might have been wiser.

No, he never had cold feet
—not a chance he'd run shoeless;
his "pillows of clay" out only
for removal; mine, out merely
for reconnaissance, relish
the chill.

My cold feet do cause me
to withdraw—I don't mean
from more pickles but
in the middle of the night,
something I write and send,
I may very well withdraw
(maybe it's the pickles
that bizarrely make me fickle)
in time before the response
I fear worse than the cold
catapults me out the door—like a
reality intruder showing up.

## Wholeness

I often wait at my email app
for mere morsels, which
I am happy to get, seeing
as no one has time for more.

Sign this petition, donate,
do your part, tell everyone
you know, here is the script,
fill out this itty-bitty survey.

In the meantime, I may sip
my java or crack a nut, walnuts
the best. But morsels even from
a nut may not suffice.

I'd like a whole piece, please.
And so I've tried to find a strategy,
thinking of nuts as people and
what it takes to explode them.

Cracking against a seam may
be like pulling apart two people
holding arms and hands tight, and
so provide the merest crumbs.

In their face could cause a snap, with,
if human, sprays of bloody tidbits
whereas walnuts—due to buffer-
under-shell—might divulge larger morsels.

The guts, or lower abdomen,
weak in either man or walnut,
is where the knot is looser bound, and
a punch could implode them almost clean.

Yet might it not be smoother just to sidle
along the seam; pressing gently...
eschewing crassness, nudging with humble
human kindness...opening all?

With the walnut's scant resemblance
to us humans, except the part that looks a lot
like brain, I'm hoping we'll be mindful
of our wholeness—if in walnut
or in man.

**Flies 2014**
(Nod to Joe Friday)

On another day these flies
would really annoy me,
but, not having found the swatter,
there was a color chart I used instead.
Lots of flies down in a general blitz—
couldn't say which fly was hit with what color.
The important thing—it was color did the trick.
The chart was browns and tans and
greys—patio tints—the ones I wouldn't
apply.  But, as it turns out,
applying the chart was dead on.

It worked well. The flies
didn't succeed in bothering me.
I learned about flies:  they can be sleepy,
incompetent, fast or slow getaway,
unexpectedly attracted to vinegar,
inclined to hang in one place,
buzz around friends' corpses.
I can kill several with one swoop,
notice nothing about them is pretty;
I can deny any glory to the one fly on the wall
stealing secrets;  I claim a clear right
to render them lifeless, forget the
foreign taboos.... I may stick them on pinheads,
for trophies.

## The birds have returned

The birds have returned in time for spring
but so too the snow.
It seems they see no place to stop
as they circle in the mirror of my laptop.
The snow will just not go
and my cursor hovers nervous over tabs.

## A lightening bug upon my shoulder

A lightening bug upon my shoulder
starts to rhythmically wink, silently
suggesting an inveigling tune;

attuned, I make a duo slinking
low notes while he, prinking,
keeps on chiming high;

agitation thus engendered jigs
his wing-tips left to right, right and left my
shoulders twitching, feet a-twinkling
he in flight!

Yes, we skipped the light fantastic, sync-ing torsos,
wings and feet; now our hearts are both a-twitter
in this spirit dance with blinks.

## Fainthearted flies 2015

Last year, much as I might prefer
not to kill all the flies alighted blitz-like
in my house, I finally had to do it.
This year's flies, with just a little prodding,
flew obliging out the window, opened only
briefly to ensure they'd not return.

Last year, they were determined to stay
even at risk of death—buzzing as in
a frenzy.  This year's brood, waiting
for my tap-tap signal they should go,
paused slightly almost saluting before
dipping blithely into the blue.

It's oftentimes a wonder how and where
they hatch—are they emanations of one's soul?
Last year, I myself felt more feisty, eager
for challenges, buzzing. This year, biding my time,
I seem to have breezed through August,
a cool window prompting me gently beyond.

**Evening star**

A neighbor in the back beyond the trees
some 200 ft. away has bought, I believe,
a large TV, regularly emitting—slightly beyond
clarity—grand illuminated arcs
as from a palace or sheik's tent, or from a
manger where one might envision
a saviour's second coming.

On yonder street, portentously called Alhambra,
slippery shadows meander toward dreamy
Moorish gardens, or airy, now Christian, arcades,
discerned through plumes of trees, no doubt
more graceful than my own scraggly arborvitae.

This neighbor doesn't know the glow
is tantalizing the others, who may wonder
if they too should buy the same.... Or demand
a visual impact study.... In my case I question
whether mellow antique shades should be allowed
to intertwine with high-contrast reality adventures,
or sacred effervescences with
pool parties or hotel conflagrations.

Broadcasters surely foresaw with glee the phantasmagoric
effect of this new market infringement—but our daunted
Venus star may not be happy—even if she were employed
to align the phosphorescent emissions or to
guide forlorn camels through the desert.

Still, repurposed as a satellite, our mercurial
evening star might conceivably receive, reroute,
and regurgitate with aplomb—every kind of mish-mash;
large screens comprising blessings in disguise,
pitting neighbor next to neighbor, linking
outpost to outpost, mingling aura with aura—
opening deliberation, rebuilding friendship
forces, inciting religious understanding, possibly
confabulating extreme Scheherazade events.

**Laptop**

I never noticed how thick
the cover of my laptop is.
This evening it is also cold
though having spent the entire day
working in 90 degree temperatures!
This coolness is hard to believe.
In fact, my laptop, while I am very fond
and spend a lot of time just gazing at her,
is completely in control and very cool.
In the same way people gaze even on
their best friends without seeing them,
so, when I gaze, I'll admit I'm looking past or through.
Fortunately, she has no feelings that I can see
for me, except that she is really quite loyal
and does let me get away with taking
minimal care of her, as when
her battery needs recharging.
Well, I suppose my noting her thickness
would be like noticing bulges where unexpected,
or density—undetectable before.
And here I have the bad manners to actually
point it out. Will this affect our relationship? Perhaps
it will ingratiate me as being more attentive, but
density cannot be flattering in any sense.
Surely my computer knows I've said this, as I am
writing the words right on her face, yet so far
and still in complete control, she has coolly
not reacted.

**Mirror on the wall**

I've had this mirror hanging
around and not on the wall,
for quite a while. I've had to think
long and hard before piercing
the wallpaper to make way for
the dubitable screws. A mirror
aping one made in India for some
ancient temple, peculiarly recalling
Italian baroque, it coordinated with the
wall's gold, plume-like border—about
a foot over where it would go.

I hardly had the courage
for the piercings, and wasn't sure
I'd hold the level straight. At
last I came to see, the screws were
not the right ones, though my friends,
embarrassed by the spider threads
observed in the supine mirror,
were sure they'd do the trick. Mirrors
break...; this too explains my languor
(and abhorrence!) 'til one day while
searching, an enigmatic hardware man
invoked a magic "monkey hook"
to give me hope—and resolution:

Screws and nails are worthless
without wood, he said, but piercing
can be done with monkeys who'll hold
on—legs and arms. Picture two wily
monkeys behind your wall—reaching out
a hand to hold up the mirror faithfully
to yourself or to whoever else walks by—
even Hanuman himself—spiders be shooed!

The mirror new, and odd in its niche
opposite the stair of my kitchen, finally

adapted to the reflected tiles, the lucky
peach in gold trim frame, the flower vase,
the frequent loping of limbs descending....

It seemed to wink when I approached
inserting my earrings..., probably assuming
we were celebrating a piercing—the compliant
monkeys chattering silently, not to be heard
at all.

## Writing is my therapy

Writing is my therapy
so I'd best sit down and
write—hurry or this moment
of need may pass, energies
dissipate, and I'll have nothing
to show for my pains. It should
be just a matter of exploring
hurts…, but I recall in my youth
an adamantly wise dorm crone
offering me two pieces of insight
all in one interim conversation:

"Dwelling on your feelings
will only make them
worse," and "When a woman
my age wants a piece of
lamb, why she wants a
piece of lamb!" Of course,

wanting a lamb chop, a simple
basic urge, may not be worth
exploring unless the chop
is on the lamm somewhere—making for
intrigue in the pursuit, or again,
in the tricky removal from the lamb…,
or, mutatis mutandi, intrigue
in the flight from mutilation.

I wanted to respect the lady,
After all she had white hair, and
heaven knows I needed counsel on
how to escape dismemberment…feeling
oddly surrounded by wolves—she herself
perhaps a wolf of sheepish allure!

I couldn't hide behind a reception
desk all day, and 'til dinner, at least,
I could engage in chatter, try to find
a path of inquiry sufficiently safe
to keep at bay for now
the wolfish reverberations.

To explore my feelings would have
been to invite controversy.
Better to imbibe her downstream wisdom,
more quickly quenching, even if somehow
phantasmagorically acrid.

I have realized it's not a matter of
exploring feelings here and now,
but those remembered as they float
past while you gulp your bubbly, and
wisdom you never thought much of
becomes enshrined while ebbing passion
exudes a subtle tinge of excitement
or a friable frisson of fear.

Still, one might hope there were profundity
in moments like these where one might seek
and find, however accidentally,
better garnished lamb chops.

(Apologies to Wordsworth and Aesop)

## Surprise of the flies 2016

This year, a surprise...no sign of
summer flies, until—there they were—
all dead on the upstairs bathroom floor,
a murky black doily shadowing
the heat duct on the wall.

Wondered not so much where they
came from, but how they passed....
Peroxide left open? vent's sharp edges?
the lacy grid and that unctuous toilet water...
ideal setting for a ritual farewell?

Later, again surprise! A horde of flies arrived
indignant, not finding their kinsmen or remains,
buzzing and peering out the kitchen window.

I crushed them with a mint-green box lid...,
too upset to devise a more decorous good-bye.

# Author's profile

I always start with my natonality—Italian, then I go to my husband's nationality—German, then I go to my college major—languages, then, these days, I leap to the fact that I write poetry. Is there a logical connection? In my mind, of course there is: Languages have words and so do poems. Italy is the land of art, poetry being an art. Germany is the land of discipline, and poetry is a disciplined art.... Is it very disciplined? To me it is disciplined to the extent that it reflects a determined inner direction. I believe this is very German; think of Luther who gambled his chance for salvation on precisely ninety-five points.

My main compulsion has always been to verbalize, and as I get older, this becomes even more clear. Just as much as when I came to America as a chatty five-year-old, or when holding court as a teen on my porch after a Halloween party, as much as when writing side-splitting dialogues with a partner for a French assignment, I love to talk and discuss, oftentimes about the meaning of words. My professional work has had to do with teaching words, writing words, reorganizing words, substituting words, and now I write lyrics with the hope of enchanting others, as much as I myself am enchanted—by words.

You may think this a very general or abstract self-presentation, but I have to ask, what else do you really need to know about a poet?

L.K., December 2016